Late Nights and Summer Storms

Amanda Pippel

BookLeaf Publishing

Presentation by *BookLeaf Publishing*

Web: www.bookleafpub.com

E-mail: info@bookleafpub.com

ISBN: 9789357442893

First edition 2023

to the summer sun, never hide your light

ACKNOWLEDGEMENT

Going into my last year of high school I knew I wanted to publish a book. The question was how? Looking back, the question really should have been who? As a new author I never realized how much work goes into a book like this and I couldn't have done it without those who supported me, no matter how small they may think that support was.

To start off, I want to thank you, the reader, for reading this book. I never expected to have anyone besides my closest friends read my work so the fact that you are here, reading it, means the world to me. I hope some of my poems can help you as much as they helped me.

Next, I want to thank my parents. Throughout my life you always let my creativity run wild (even when it was a bit chaotic, sorry about the dog bowl perfume). Your support of my imagination has helped inspire so much of my work.

I also want to thank my sibling for all the late night venting and wrestling on the floor. You have always been there for me and your wonderful (yet dark) sense of humor always makes me laugh.

I've also got to thank my grandparents for their support (and the $50), I couldn't have done this without you (literally).

Then, I have to thank the sun and stars to my moon, you know who you are. You always shine when things look dark and balance me out. I'm gonna miss you guys at school.

Next, I've got to thank all of my school friends: Hampton, Callie, Kaitlyn, Sanae, and sort of Steven (it counts). I'll always remember the goldfish, late night DnD sessions, truth or truth, tooby milk, and so much more. You guys all kept me sane, even when we didn't act like it.

I need to add in a quick thanks to some teachers too. Ms. Geeslin, thank you for sparking my love for poetry and prose, I never would have written my first poem if it weren't for you. Mr. Gritter, thank you for the free writes that kept my creative juices flowing. Mr. Ramsey, thank you for the deep conversations and for caring about my passions (btw you should cook something with elderberry and breadcrumbs). Mr. Leibel, thank you for helping me improve my writing and for giving me a chance to defend half-rhymes.

Lastly, I want to thank Book Leaf Publishing for this opportunity (and Instagram for your scarily good advertising), as well as Edgar Allen Poe for his relatable poems and A Cask of Amontillado. His work will stick with me forever.

It all started with a shoe...

that first night,
when was it?
3rd grade?

back on that day,
when i first saw your face,
what month was it, may?

but who cares who…

that first night,
where was it?
kirkland?

out near the sand,
that bustling, private place,
i held onto your hand,

but who cares where…

that first night,
what was it?
a lake?

there in the wake,
drawings we later erase,
the memories we make,

but who cares what…

that first night,
why was it?
just fate?

always slightly late,
those minutes lost in space,
it felt like forever, i'd wait,

but who cares why…

who cares when?
who cares where?
who cares what?
who cares why?
all start with the same question… who

that first night,
who was it?
you

the first signs of dew,
pressed flowers, hearts start to race,
my love born anew

but who cares who…
I do

longing

everyone longs for something
some for the sun
others for the moon
or the stars

many long for a person
some for a place
others for a feeling
or a time

i don't know what i long for
although i think it's many things
for i know some of them

i long for the night
to see their face again
for a perfect song
or the right words to say
i long for expression
and clarity of mind
for something that fits me
or a reason in life
i long for that friendship
to say what i feel
for youthful exuberance
or a story to tell

i long for so much
but there is always something...
missing

i have this void
in my soul
i long-
i long-
to fill it...

but how?

home

they say home is where the heart is,
well if that's true my home is you,

i've never felt a strong connection to a place,
no area that always makes me feel safe,
but wherever you are, i do,

i want to be your home

i don't have to be the only one
i think people can have multiple,

a place you go to cry,
a person you tell everything to,
an item that reminds you
of your happiest days,

everyone needs a home

these aren't just platitudes
said to fill
an obligatory hole,
something to make it all feel real,

because it is real,
all of it,
it's real to me,
is it real to you?

if home is where the heart is
and god, i hope that's true,
i just need you to know
i'm home when i'm with you

love me pretty

pretty is more than an adjective to me
it's a feeling
an emotion
it's a flower crown nestled in my dark hair
it's a plaid skirt with my rose docs
it's small braids in their hair
or the smile that they make
when i finally see their face
traces of warm air after a summer's rain
pretty is how i feel for those i love
pretty is how the words feel as they roll off my
tongue
pretty is what keeps me going
falling into their arms
waiting for their words
"Pretty"
they whisper in my ears
and i smile, happy, content,
pretty

art

you remember that poem
they wrote about you
in the back of
your mind. it lingers

as you both wander
hand in hand. no. their hand
lingers, air, heat, near
your side as it hangs
and you let it lie

because you don't notice
as your eyes drift
around the room. art
surrounds you, consumes you
your eyes light up, shining
in the evening light as
you wander, hand
near hand. close
but not... touching

but they don't care
as their hand stays, to
remind you
they are there

too. and they
are surrounded by art
yet consumed by
you.

mirrors

you feel trapped in
your own skin always
looking, glancing
in the mirrors you walk by
but not seeing yourself
never really feeling
yourself
but you see this
beautiful girl
staring, blinking
back at you, confused
lost, lonely
like you but
not you

pretty

there is nothing i love more
than the word
pretty

the soft love
of encompassing warmth
flowers, sun, pretty

not beautiful
not extravagant
just simple

just pretty

so please
call me
pretty

hiwblgong

i doubt you remember this
but it doesn't matter
it still reminds me
of talking to you
every single day

i'd say it's kinda like
your signature thing
keysmashing is an art when it comes to you
no sense in letters
but it expresses it right
the emotions
and i can relate to how you feel

you know
i kinda miss it
the games in the summer
all the memories
but we're making new ones
and that's okay

just please
never forget me

us

this is a big step
into futures we always wanted
but never expected we'd have
never thought it would actually
come

some people move on
some stay
which ones are we?

i say i'll always remember
but will i?
will we
remember everything

i say i'll text
but will i?
will we
ever speak again

in 20 years
10 years
5 years
1 year
will any of this matter
anymore?

will any of us matter
anymore?

i don't want to grow apart
but should i?
should we?

is that the first step
to a life we always wanted
but never expected we'd have
never thought would actually
come

i don't want to miss you
i don't want to miss us

do you think about me?

        most nights
i lie awake
          wondering
if you
             do
too

i know you do

i hope it's a cold sweat
        you're sleeping in now
as you lie awake
        with me on your mind
tossing and turning
        wondering why you
ever let me go

summer sun

lying in the summer sun
your hand rests in mine,
lying in the summer sun
no clouds in the sky,

lying in the summer sun
hair on the seats,
lying in the summer sun
i'm never gonna leave,

lying in the summer sun
looking in your eyes,
lying in the summer sun
pictures of you and i,

lying in the summer sun
trees up above,
lying in the summer sun
the day i fell in love

night

when you lie there
warm and safe
in the glistening starlit night
where does your mind wander?

does the dark
creep in on you?
as the stars burn out
one
by
one

do your thoughts
turn against you?
one
by
one

when you lie there
cold and alone
in the darkening starless night
do you ask yourself if you're okay?

are you okay?

constellations

when you gaze upon the many stars
in the lonely midnight sky
you heart draws you pictures
of what is on your mind

when you gaze upon the many stars
in the lonely midnight sky
does your heart draw you pictures
of your hand in mine?

why

sometimes
i'm just sad
that's it
just that overwhelming
sense of despair
nostalgia maybe
sometimes grief
for something i never had
but i get sad
and i just want to cry
i want to break down
and scream
and laugh through my hysteria
and got i just
don't know why

alone

sometimes
you just want to be alone
with your thoughts
with your pain
but you can't
you're trapped
and you just want
out

leave me alone

you know you're okay
you just need a
break

please just let me be alone

but never lonely

this poem goes out
to all the people
who made me realize
it's okay to be alone
it's okay to feel sad
to show your emotions
and even deal with it on your own,
but to the people who showed me
i don't have to,
thank you
for letting me be alone,
but never lonely

silence

i don't know
what to write
so i scream
into the abyss
that is
my mind
and write down
the hollow words
that are left
behind

numb

i use so many words
to describe my feelings
in my eloquent fashion
i can move a room
with just my emotions
but what do i do
when i can't?

what do i do
when i just feel nothing?
empty
numb

how do you describe
the void that fill you?
takes up every spot
hiding in every corner

how do you explain
when you have nothing left to say?
when the words are gone
when you just feel alone

even when you're surrounded by people
when you know that they care

but you just can't bring yourself
to spill out the nothing inside

how do you relate
when there is nothing inside
to relate to?
when all you are is gone
incomplete
missing
what is left to share?

what is left or them to see?
what is left for them to love?

what is left... of you?

rain

words have such strong connotations
but they shift
with context
with different people
and sometimes
rain is sad
at the same time
it's a life giving spring day
but it's the anger of thunder
and the soft trickle of sunlit gray
and you never know which
rain you'll get
but it's always the same
comfort on a lonely day
pure to wash your fears away
and maybe you're a different person
but i love it
even when it makes me want to cry and scream
because rain is complex
and maybe it helps me discover
some of its complexity in me

late nights and summer storms.

when you hear the faint
tapping of rain
and the dark light
of an evening's love
filters through your room
you realize
there really is nothing like
the comfort you can find
in late nights and summer storms.